MATHEMATICAL PROOFS
THAT
GOD EXISTS

Power to Create

Power to Punish

God Exists

Patrocel N. Duque

ISBN 0-7414-3975-1

Published by:

INFINITY
PUBLISHING.COM

1094 New DeHaven Street, Suite 100
West Conshohocken, PA 19428-2713
Info@buybooksontheweb.com
www.buybooksontheweb.com
Toll-free (877) BUY BOOK
Local Phone (610) 941-9999
Fax (610) 941-9959

Printed in the United States of America

Printed on Recycled Paper

Published January 2008

A Friendly Notice

This book:

+Will show how philosophers, theologians, mathematicians, and scientists from the ancient period through the middle ages and up to modern times attempted and are trying to decipher the Creator's identity and dimensions.

Is this book an answer to the thousands of years search for the illusive divine equations? Through this book, you may judge for yourself.

+Will not replace your faith but will instead reinforce it. It is for all regardless of faith and nonfaith, believers and nonbelievers.

+Is meant not only for mathematicians but also for non-mathematicians. Mathematical portions are also explained in simple terms and illustrations.

+Is for all regardless of profession, vocation, education, age, race or gender.

+Is unique. Something new. Informative. Creative. At times entertaining.

A rational way to reinforce the faith of believers.
A convincing method to make nonbelievers acknowledge Him.

Dedication

Foremost, I dedicate this labor of love to You, Lord who motivated and inspired me to start and continue the pursuit of Your divine commission - to make the whole humanity acknowledge and believe in You as Creator and Savior.

I express my utmost gratitude for bestowing Your blessings upon those people who supported and are helping in this noble crusade to spread Your Gospel through a rational approach to the minds and hearts of men and women across the world. Many of those who have a hand in the making of this book are now enjoying the blessings that Thou art generously gifting out.

As this crusade undertakes its mission, please continue to bless those who are supportive and bless also the readers of this book who shall be Your future devout servants to carry on the torch of Your Divine Call.

*All of these I dedicate for Your glory and ultimate triumph as Maker with the unlimited power of **Infinity**.*

The Divine Equations

Date:

Address:

My Gift to:

_____

_____

_____

_____

Giver

"God Loves a Cheerful Giver."

Table of Contents

Preface

*My experiences have shown me that life truly is a
journey and the less baggage we carry,
the easier the ride.*

Wally Amos

This book is about **Infinity** and **heavens**. It may
be of interest to mention here that I searched for so
many long hours and days through the Internet and went
through some fifty publishers world-wide. Then I came
across a publisher that called my attention. Aside from
its good offers, the following aroused my curiosity. Its
name: **Infinity** Publishing.com and its address:
DeHaven St. Could these be coincidences or Divine
guidance?

As you read through, there are more coincidences
or Divine interventions to unfold.

You are now going to start a new yet
enlightening journey in your life. It is not a physical
travel but one that will engage your eyes, mind and
heart all at the same time. It will start at point A and
ends at point Z. Your travel will take you step by step
like learning a new alphabet, from A to B, C, and so on.
As you go through the steps, please read and understand
carefully; do not speed-read. Savor this experience.
After some parts or chapters, there is a blank scenery
page. Pause, close your eyes and ponder what you have
read or gone through. Imagine yourself as part of any
scene around you....a tree, a rock or anything else.
After which continue reading.

Stories are interspersed in the discussion to emphasize some points. It is made this way because parables linger longer in the mind than plain words.

As you read, you will come across the mathematical illustrations which are presented in understandable format. Should you have an aversion to mathematical symbols and figures, please skip them and just read the literature that explains the meaning as well.

At the end of the book, there is a survey form which I request you to fill up and mail to me. This will serve as my guide in my future publications which I plan to work on in order to benefit more our readers. Please be patient enough to accomplish the form because it will help me adjust or add on things to enable me to attain an aspiration: to reach out to everyone – believers and nonbelievers worldwide in the best way possible.

This book may be a good gift to your beloveds, friends or even your enemies (to win them to your side). There is a page for this purpose.

At the end of your journey, there is a finale scene. Imagine yourself as part of a panoramic scene recalling these words from David Belasco: *"When God conceived the world, that was poetry. He formed it and that was sculpture. He colored it and that was painting. He peopled it with living things and that was grand, eternal, divine drama."*

See you then at point Z, hopefully, an enlightened and renewed person.

Enjoy your trip. Bon voyage!

Why I Wrote This Book

I

*This is true: Give the best in everything you do,
and more than the best will return to you.*

— The Author

*"ABANDON SHIP!!! ALL HANDS ABANDON
SHIP!!!" ordered the helpless captain of the sinking
ship.*

*Everyone did his best to save the ship but to no
avail. It was beyond human ability and endurance. The
vessel was doomed to sink at any moment.*

*People on board the ship were shouting and
crying for God's help, while the others were dead silent
inside their cabins where they were closeted, and the rest
were hysterical, having lost their wits waiting for death
to overcome them. The chilly weather, waves as tall as
five-story buildings and winds gusting to more than 100
miles per hour were buffeting the ship caught in the midst
of a rampaging super typhoon in one of the most
turbulent water channels of the world. The captain of the
ship already ordered "Abandon ship" but where would
these officers, crew members and passengers go? Earlier
pandemonium indeed broke loose. That was almost an
hour ago. If they stayed inside their cabins, they would
surely sink with the ship. Thus they rushed to the open
deck but all of them were washed away by the rampaging
winds and waves. It was pitch dark, the engines of the
ship stopped, and there were no lights on board. The
vessel was sinking fast.*

The remaining seamen scampered outside from their cabins only to be swept away too by the winds and waves to the tumultuous and angry open sea.

"I prayed and shouted for God's help," recalled one of the few survivors. "I cried for God to spare our lives.

"Leo, my close friend and bunkmate, was with me throughout the whole ordeal. When the vessel was in an upright position, we rushed to the open deck. We climbed up the bridge located at the tallest floor of the ship which was the captain's command control center. As we entered, we saw the captain heavily drenched in rain and sea water looking haggard and desperate trying to figure out how we could escape from the nature's fury. His once jovial disposition was the opposite of what he was at that moment.

"He ordered us, 'Tie me to this ship!' He was holding a half-inch nylon rope and motioning us to tie his body to a protruding metal post.

"'Sir, let's go! The ship will sink anytime now!' we pleaded.

"'No! Tie me to this ship!!' We saw his stern face, commanding yet pleading us at the same time. His once youthful face turned years older. We felt deep respect and great pity for him that we could not leave him to his death alone. It occurred to my mind: 'How could I leave our captain who was so fatherly to us in all the years we were together aboard ship?' We just could not let him sink with this ship. He was like my father whom I would offer my life in time of need. Now, it was not only a need – it was a sure death. We should try to save him instead. But I saw in his face the depth and urgency of his message. It was his wish – a plea to vindicate his honor. I realized that a captain of a ship has the deep sense of duty to put the lives of his men and passengers foremost than his own. He must save the ship at all cost or sink with it. It is an honorable tradition of sea-going captains.

"With a heavy heart I motioned Leo to help me tie him. It was his last wish. As we were tying him, I saw a glimpse of hope in his teary and bloodshot eyes. We, too, cried while we were tying him. He knew that when the typhoon would subside, the ship would remain afloat and he would still be on this ship....tied....dead or alive. Or sink with it.

"As soon as we finished tying him, huge waves and tornado-like winds almost capsized our ship. Leo was thrown and was slammed hard to the metal wall; I was lucky the captain and I were locked in tight embrace. He was already tightly fastened to the metal post. We held on to each other as tightly as we could.

"When the ship was in an upright position again, our captain pleaded: 'Sons, you get out of here. Seek cover somewhere down!' As I called for Leo, he was already gone and I did not see him anymore. He was flushed out by the rushing tons of waters and tossed away by the gigantic waves and powerful winds. The rushing water instantly filled up to the eight-foot ceiling of the bridge-room that kept us momentarily underwater. We were being drowned slowly but surely. As the ship went upright again, waters rushed out quickly. These were the continuous and furious flow and ebb of waters. Weeping, I bade our beloved captain a quick goodbye. I felt that I myself dug the grave of my father to be buried alive. But that was his final wish – an honorable desire of a brave man...his last stand as a noble and ultimate warrior.

"He shouted again, 'Son, take cover. Go! God... please save us!!' I rushed downward to seek refuge.

"All of a sudden a huge wave swept me from the open deck. I did not feel anything anymore. Was I dying? The wave carried me for so long and I was floating and flying in this total darkness. Then I felt that I was dead. God abandoned me!"

A day passed. The storm left behind death and devastation.

"I woke up and I was surprised I was in this place. Who brought me here? I felt excruciating pains all over my body; I could not move. I tried hard to recall what happened. As the sun broke through the skies, I looked around and I was on this shore. Slowly, I recalled that incident when our ship was sinking. I rejoiced that God saved me. What about my friends? I looked around and realized that I was alone. God loves me! But where was Leo? What about our beloved captain? I wept like a child."

This was my interview with one of the few survivors of that ill-fated ship that sank in the northern tip of the Philippines some two decades ago. The captain of the ship who perished was my good friend. Out of the more than two hundred officers, crew members, and passengers on board, only a dozen survived.

The ship was caught in the center of a super typhoon in the Balintang Channel, a strait in the northern tip of the Philippines where the might of the two huge oceans merge – the China Sea and the Pacific Ocean. Even in fair weather it is still the most feared water in the world because of being turbulent in nature.

By chance, I was fortunate to interview this seaman, one of the very few survivors. I was then searching for a true-to-life experience that I used in my speech in a nationwide competition of the Toastmasters International Club. I was the regional representative in the speech and song contests (I won in the song category instead; in real life it is almost impossible to win them all).

This sinking incident left an indelible mark in my heart and mind that I kept on thinking about why people procrastinate and have to wait for a life-or-death situation to overwhelm them before they acknowledge and accept God. The sailor I interviewed mentioned in passing that prior to the tragedy he thought God had not existed or he just had not prayed before. It was only during that ill-fated incident that he was convinced that God was saving him.

As for the believers who unfortunately perished, most likely they accepted their fate and surrendered to the Creator with happy spirits. God must have welcomed them in heaven where they are now happily resting eternally. It is along this thought that I usually ask myself: Where do nonbelievers go after death? Is it their fault that they did not believe in the Creator?

At this juncture, let me ask the nonbeliever: Do you have to wait for a life-or-death scenario to make you decide whether or not you believe in God? That will be a difficult choice indeed. When you are in that situation you have no other option but to believe in Him. You cannot do otherwise. So why wait? I could not blame them. Perhaps no one explained to them the peace and beauty of believing God. Nobody opened their minds and hearts to accepting God as the most cherished thing that could ever happen to them.

Of the more than six billion humans on earth, statistics show, which I will present later, that more than two billion souls probably do not believe in Him. Could it be because of their cultures, their upbringing, their ways of life? So it's not the fault of the nonbelievers themselves that they are so. They may be just victims of their own environment or the lifestyles of their parents or guardians. Could some of them be the intellectual elites who cannot harmonize science with faith or vice versa?

I searched for the answer to these questions that kept nagging me since that fateful incident.

Suddenly, the key to the answer flashed through my mind: Convince the nonbelievers that there is God and make the believers reinforce their faith with this gem of thought – a mathematical equation I learned in high school.

But along the way, I felt intimidated. I am neither a good writer, nor a preacher, nor an academician. I am a simple professional soldier. I have not written a single book, except for some articles, poems, songs and short stories in newspapers and magazines. How could I correlate this equation to theology? Could I be understood by any ordinary person or layman?

I searched in libraries but to my perception, there are not many articles persuasive enough to convince the nonbelievers or to reinforce further the faith of the believers in concrete and tangible terms. Many are based on faith or "just trust your preachers." You can convince the faithful, no doubt, but how about the nonbelievers?

For almost five years, I consulted friends, some of whom are mathematicians, and little by little I "discovered" how to correlate mathematics to religion.

God Touched Me

Sometime in May 2006, God touched me. I was awakened at around two o'clock in the morning. It was not my usual waking time. Oddly enough, I felt the urgency to start on the book because I was apprehensive that if I did otherwise, I might lose my desire and forget all about it…. like a dream. I earnestly prayed to God to set my frame of mind aright with the ability to do it. It seemed that an angel directed me to walk to my office, sit on my chair, grab a pen and sheets of paper. It was so difficult for me to start writing the core of my thesis for the last five years. But that morning, I found it so easy and finished it in a little over an hour. Strangely, I felt that the hand of God guided me. I did not realize that my years of searching and procrastination would be resolved so quickly. The remaining chapters supporting these equations from then on were just as easy to write. God touched my heart and mind!

In due time, I will be able to publish this book which I dedicate to all, especially to the nonbelievers who are missing out the best things that they have yet to know and to the believers to enable them to reinforce their faith and sustain them for as long as they live. They serve as my inspirational backdrop – the people of the world. Wouldn't it be great to reach out to them? It is an impossible dream but my faith coupled with modern technology will make the barrier less impossible. As of this writing, May 29, 2006 according to the US Census Bureau on World Population Clocks – POP Clocks there are 6, 518, 923, 052 people on earth. Hereunder is the breakdown of religions of the world in 2000, which includes their adherents, rankings and percentages of the world's total religions. These data are from the *Encyclopedia Britannica.*

Going through these significant data, we see that there are still countless souls in the dark. These more than six billion souls are God's best creation. Since we are included here, let us therefore treasure, love and reach out to one another.

As you go through the subsequent pages, please take my brotherly advice: "Your minds and hearts are just like parachutes, they function only when open."

Religion	Population	Percent (%)	Rank
1) Christians **(total of a-e)**	1,955,229,000	33.7	1
a)Roman Catholics	981,465,000	16.9	
b)Protestants	404,020,000	7.0	
c)Orthodox	218,350,000	3.8	
d)Anglicans	69,136,000	1.2	
e)Other Christians	282,258,000	4.9	
2) Muslims	1,126,325,000	19.4	2
3) Nonreligious	886,929,000	15.3	3
4) Hindus	793,076,000	13.7	4
5) Buddhists	325,275,000	5.6	5
6) Atheists	222,195,000	5.6	6
7) Chinese folk religionists	220,971,00	3.8	7
8) New Religionists	106,016,000	1.8	8
9) Ethnic Religionists	102,945,000	1.8	9
10) Sikhs	19,508,000	0.3	10
11) Jews	13,866,000	0.2	
12) Spiritists	10,293,000	0.2	
13) Baha'is	6,404,000	0.1	
14) Confucians	5,086,000	0.1	
15) Jains	4,920,000	0.1	
16) Shintoists	2,898,000	--	
17) Other Religionists	1,952,000	--	
18) Parsees	191,000	--	
19) Mandeans	45,000	--	

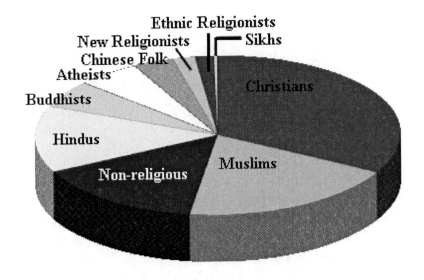

Top 10 World Religions

Although Christianity is the majority, it is clear by the chart that many divisions are included. Criteria generally used for polling simply asked for personal profession of religion – not actual participation or exercise of belief system.

How Will This Book Benefit the Reader?

II

*Many good ideas are discovered between
the writer's pen and the readers' eyes.*

—The Author

It is not usual that a chapter or a prime part of a book is titled in a question. It is purposely done this way to engage the mind and heart of the reader first before continuing on. The title raises the questions: "Will this be beneficial to me as a believer or a nonbeliever of a Creator or God? Will this affect my quest for a true God? Will this reinforce my faith? Will this make me a better person?"

Before I publish this book, I distributed typewritten pamphlets to some people for a small survey. The question asked was: "In a scale of 0 to10 (0 is nonbeliever while 10 is strong believer), how strong now is your belief in the Creator or God?" A few days after reading the pamphlet, I repeated the same question. Here are the results:

Names	Before Reading	After Reading
Rodger	8	9.5
Lydia	10	12*
Angie	9	9.5
Pete	7.5	12*
Fredy	10	13*
Benny	7	11*
Louie	10	11*

Med	10	13*
Sheila	9.5	12*
Larry	7	12*
Joe	10	12*
Lory	10	12*
Brent	8	9.5
Betty	7	11*

*In excess of 10 means that their faith had been more than reinforced than expected and went beyond the standard scale of 10.

The survey was conducted in Guam, USA which has a population of 160,000. The people are predominantly Christians or almost all are believers of a creator. It is very seldom that there are atheists or nonbelievers in the mainstream of religions on the island.

It would have been better had I met nonbelievers. Although I am hoping that there are none in my midst but if I meet them I will gladly include them in my continuing survey. Because of time constraints, these are just the initial results. I will publish the more comprehensive results in subsequent editions.

Let us analyze the results as shown in the table.

These people could be classified into three categories.

1. Strong believers – Those at scale 10.
2. Varied believers – Those with varying degrees of beliefs from scale 1 to 9.
3. Nonbelievers – Those at scale 0.

It is observed that the strong believers' beliefs were reinforced on the average by 22%, while the varied believers were reinforced by 33%. These percentages are the "reinforcibility" of this book. Take the case of those who are in the scale of 7 to 7.5. The average increase is 62%. Therefore, the lower the varied believers' position in the scale, the greater is this thesis's "reinforcibility." As for the nonbelievers who are at the lowest scale, I perceive that the "convincibility" of the book will be much higher.

When the manuscripts were distributed to the survey participants, the book was only 70% complete. Now, with more chapters and illustrations added and with God's grace, the thesis's "reinforcibility" and "convincibility" will be much more. It therefore could have more positive impact especially to the nonbelievers.

The transformations of the participants occurred in an average reading time of six hours, complete with pauses and afterthoughts.

As you read this outcome, the book will most likely do the same thing for you: it will increase or reinforce your faith or will not confuse you. It will open to you a new path not trod before. Experience for yourself as a newly rediscovered person in the most memorable and pleasant way, just as you came from your classroom having mentally absorbed your new lessons. Reading this book now may just be like a trip to the laboratory for some pragmatic experimentations and new applications.

For those who have apprehension to mathematical symbols, I have presented this book in a more easily understandable format. Should you still have an aversion to mathematical figures, skip them but read the literature, which explains as well the meaning of the figures and the results.

When you read "The Power to Create", please take note of the computation on how Jesus was able to feed around 5,000 followers from the original five loaves of bread. Try doing the computation and you will find it interesting. Want to feed 10,000? 20,000? Try to do it yourself as if you were in the shoes of Jesus feeding your own followers. It is just learning His ways by doing them (A word of caution though: Please do not attempt to do this when you are hosting a party, especially in a hotel. You may be embarrassed or get your credit records discredited).

As I relate parables and stories, I acknowledge the original writers, but with so many sources, (i.e. Internet, magazines, newsletters, books, movies, etc.), it is impossible for me to recall them all. Some stories were passed through word-of-mouth. If I failed to recall their origins, may the original authors understand my situation. To them, I owe acknowledgements.

As you read, there are some words or sentences that are enclosed in brackets [ ] and others are paraphrased. These words are mine and I wrote them for emphasis and clarity. To protect the privacy of individuals and organizations, I modified some incidents. Any similarities of circumstances are coincidental.

In going through life, have you ever thought that there might be something that you are missing out? Are you happy with what you are now? What I will explain may give you some answers on how you are created. Welcome to the realm of the *Divine Proportion*.

Divine Proportion

The *divine proportion* is also called the golden number, rule or ratio. It was discovered during the 12th century AD by the greatest European mathematician of the middle ages, the Italian Leonardo Fibonacci. It is called the "*phi*" with a value of 1.618. During the early years and up to modern times, many are fascinated with its unusual mathematical properties. Why this divine proportion? Because it is one of those mysterious and significant laws that the Creator had developed for His creation.

It is a series of numbers where each new number in the series is the sum of the two numbers before it. So the sequence goes: 1, 2, 3, 5, 8, 13....and so on. The ratio of each successive pair of numbers (i.e. 5/3, 8/5, 13/8 ....) is approximately 1.618. This proportion is observed to be true in most creation, both animate and inanimate objects.

An example is the length of a person's arm measured from the shoulder to the fingertips. If you multiply the length of your lower arm (from elbow to fingertips) by 1.618, the result is the approximate length of your entire arm.

In the usual branching of trees, the lowest starts at one which is the trunk. The next level has two branches, the third level has three branches, the fourth level has five and the subsequent levels follow the series 8, 13, 21 and so on.

The best application of this theory is the human face. The length and width of the forehead in relation to the dimension of the face conforms with this golden rule; the dimension of the nose follows the golden proportion in relation to the nostrils; the length of the nose conforms with the overall length of the face; the length of the lips in relation to their thickness and width, etc. And as for the teeth, the two front incisor teeth form golden rectangles with the *phi* ratio. In short, the width multiplied by 1.618 equals the height of a tooth. All of these proportions are observed to be intricately designed to include most parts of the human body. God must be so meticulous in designing everything in us and on earth! Amazing isn't it? Now, if you look at the mirror and your facial features are not "divinely" proportioned, you may ask your parents in good humor – "Mom and Dad, where were you when God was designing humans?"

In Exodus 25:10, Moses received God's commandments to build the Ark of the Covenant which was to hold the Ten Commandments, saying: "Have them make a chest of acacia-wood two and a half cubits long and one and a half wide and a cubit and a half high." The ratio of 2.5 to 1.5 approximates the *phi* value.

In Genesis 6:15, God commanded Noah to build an ark: "And this is how you shall make it: The length of the ark shall be three hundred cubits, its width fifty cubits and its height thirty cubits."

The front and back views of the ark formed a rectangle each with the divine proportion of 50x30 cubits. This is the value of phi, the ratio of 50 to 30.

The top view of the ark is 300x50 cubits. The whole numbers 3 and 5 are the consecutive sequence of the divine proportion series

The number *666* is also explained in terms of the *phi*.

Our readers may research further into this fascinating subject on their own time. My aim for now is to convey to the readers that our lives are governed by sets of divine mathematical equations of which we know only some. It is my hope that through time many more will be discovered. May this book open your eyes and minds to another new idea – the divine equations which prove that God exists.

SCENERY

Afterthoughts

Unknowingly, God Led Me the Way

III

The greatest tragedy in life is not death
but life that fails to fulfill its purpose and potential.

—Easter Morning Inspirations, Inc.

On an ordinary bond paper, I drew a half-inch letter "D" at the center and asked ten people at random what they saw.

Nine out of ten saw the letter "D." Only one said, "I see a white paper with a small letter 'D' at the center."

What does this mean?

The letter "D" stands for distractions or other things. People tend to focus on other things and usually overlook the overall picture.

This is the parallel to asking the question: Do you believe that God exists? People's attention is usually drawn to things that obscure their perception of the Creator.

In this world, we have the believers and nonbelievers – the atheist, agnostic, cultist, etc.

On May 28, 2006 I conducted a worldwide survey through the Internet's "Question and Answer." The reactions of the respondents throughout the world were varied, yet interesting. My question was: "How many nonbelievers of God are there in the world?"

When you ask the believers why they believe that God exists, their common answer is: It is by faith;

however, preachers usually encourage in-depth study of the Scriptures.

In 1939 Albert Einstein, in his article on religion, observed that people believe in God because of two things: reward and punishment. Reward, because they will have better lives on earth and subsequently in heaven; and punishment, because they will go to hell if they disbelieve or disobey God. Einstein said that the best way to believing God is to have rational relationship with Him.

Yes, it will be a more lasting belief that way. Father Raniero Contalamessa, in a Vatican Lenten sermon, said that even committed believers struggle to obey the Lord. He said that their love of God is often like a "tree planted along city street; the struggle (belief in God) grows cracks in the sidewalk."

To my mind, this could be overcome by reinforcing their faith in God with something that is not only rational but also concrete by making science or mathematics reinforce theological doctrines.

Nowadays, science and religion have much in common but there are also some disagreements. I will not discuss them here because my main intention is to present these mathematical proofs that God exists. These proofs will further reduce whatever disagreements there are among evolutionists, creationists, intelligent design (ID) proponents, Big Bang theorists, atheists, etc. regarding the real origin of human existence. As such, my ultimate goal is to spread these mathematical proofs in order to reinforce the faith of the believers and to make the nonbelievers re-evaluate their stand on God's existence; subsequently, if they realize this to be true, then God's desire is realized – that they genuinely acknowledge His power and therefore His existence. This, too, is my aspiration.

As I write this thesis, I have to be candid in revealing my "faith." Before writing this book, I was only 75 percent sure that God exists. Just like the tree, my faith cracks at the very foundation; in short, it was founded not on solid ground.

Going through the steps of the mathematical equations, little by little I realized that I was being led to "somewhere" that will reinforce my belief in God: the power to create, power to punish and ultimately His existence. In the end, I more than realized that there is a superpower who designs every creation on earth, the planets, the stars, the universe, the galaxies, the "black holes," etc. These were created or did not happen by sheer accident. They were designed and, still more, are being created by the Creator. Through my humble human perception, God showed me the way so that others may follow suit as I relate my vivid "journey" that is worth more than all of my lifetime experiences.

As we go through this academic exercise, I know that many will be curious about the interpretation of this formula. Remember that God writes "straight lines in indirect ways." He will not show us how, but instead it behooves us to figure out ways to discover this window of opportunity so that we may feel and see His power and eventually His presence. Afterwards, let's rely on Him to show us the light in ways which are beyond human imagination. How will we do it then? Only God knows as shown in this anecdote from Christopher Notes[1] which explains His intricate ways:

"The Need For Struggle"

"A man found a cocoon of the emperor moth and took it home to watch it emerge. One day a small opening appeared, and for several hours the moth struggled, but couldn't seem to force its body past a certain point.

Deciding something was wrong, the man took a pair of scissors and snipped the remaining bit of cocoon. The moth emerged easily, its body large and swollen, the wings small and shriveled.

He expected that in a few hours the wings would spread out in their natural beauty, but they did not. Instead of developing into a creature free to fly, the [poor] moth spent its life dragging around a swollen body and shriveled wings.

The constricting cocoon and the struggle necessary to pass through the tiny opening are God's ways of forcing fluid from the body into the wings. The 'merciful' snip was, in reality, cruel. [It subsequently died]. Sometimes the struggle is exactly what we need."

It is by nature that humans also choose the path of least resistance, avoiding the hard struggles as we go through life. But God provides this "survival mechanism" for us to be able to develop our immune system and ability to survive. Through nature's ways, we are unconsciously utilizing these tools for survival – so our life cycle goes on *ad infinitum* in this planet. Unknown to many, this is part of His great design.

Additionally, in our midst we encounter difficulties – we resist the way and what we perceive – refusing to change, come what may. The struggles are within ourselves. But I observe that the only permanent thing in this world is "change." As creatures, we will have to change in order to survive. God has His own unexpected ways of changing things.

Here is the gist of a parable of Bruno Hagspiel[2] about a nonbeliever who was spreading his "gospel" that God does not exist.

"Jane, I'll give you lots of candies as long as you say these words daily: 'My GOD is NOWHERE.'"

The girl tried to memorize this by heart and even learned to put melody into it.

After a week, the atheist checked on the girl to recite her words.

Radiant and smiling, Jane rejoiced as she sang the words: "My GOD is NOW HERE!"

As you read through this thesis, it is my hope that at the end, you will be like that little girl, radiant, smiling and rejoicing – yourself rediscovered, emotionally and spiritually reinforced and strengthened.

Mathematics (or Science) and Religions

IV

Laws of nature are written by the
hands of God in the language of mathematics.

– Galileo Galilei

Mathematics came from a Greek word which means "inclined to learn." It is an abstract intellectual activity that started in Greece during the 6th century BC.

Early mathematicians tried to prove that the behavior of the planet's animate and inanimate objects follow sets of pattern.

Johannes Kepler in the 16th century AD observed: "The chief aim of all investigations of the external world should be to discover the rational order and harmony which has been imposed on it by God and which He revealed to us in the language of mathematics." Moreover, another scientist-mathematician, *Morris Kline* believed "God had designed the universe and it was expected that all phenomena of nature follow one master plan. One mind designing a universe would almost surely have employed one set of basic principles to govern all related phenomena."

In the 1920s two mathematicians *S. Banach* and *A. Tarski* tried to explain how Jesus Christ was able to feed five thousand people out of five loaves of bread and two fish (Mark 6:30-56).

They came up with mathematical formula which is questioned as to its accuracy and relevance. It was therefore called the *Banach-Tarski* paradox.

In his address to the Princeton Theological Seminary in 1939, *Albert Einstein,* a great mathematician and genius said: "The further the spiritual evolution of mankind advances, the more certain it seems to me that the path to genuine religiosity does not lie through fear of life and the fear of death and blind faith, but through striving after rational knowledge."

He added, "Science without religion is lame [untamed], religion without science is blind."

In the 700-page book *"Mathematics and the Divine"* by *T. Koetsier* and *L. Bergmans,* the authors show the relationship between numbers and God, between geometric figures and religious beliefs, abstract structures vis-à-vis theological doctrines. They distinguish three periods in the relationship of mathematics and the Divine during the pre-Greek period, classical Greek period during the medieval and Renaissance reigns, thence to the modern era. They mention how mathematics were employed for religious and metaphysical reasons; allude even number six as a perfect number for God having completed His creation in six days; cite the numerological calculations that predicted the end of the world at 8 A M Oct.19, 1533. These are called the mathematization of physical phenomena that give rise to modern natural science. Other philosophers and mathematicians like Galileo Galilei and Isaac Newton tried to use mathematics as a language in deciphering God's intentions in the structure of the cosmos.

By and large this book *"Mathematics and the Divine"* provides some valuable contributions in encouraging others to explore this challenging, relatively uncharted endeavor. More often than not, science and religion are on the opposite corners of the human mind. While there might be common points of agreements, through time, there are widening gaps as man tries to decipher present-day happenings in terms of theological and mathematical phenomena, this book further states.

Intelligent Design, etc.

In the book, *"Signs of Intelligence,"* authors *W. Dembster* and *J. Kushiner* advance the belief that there is an intelligent designer that created this universe. They analyze the studies of Darwin in his thesis of evolution vis-à-vis creation; point out some weaknesses in mutation and natural selection processes as advanced by the evolutionists.

In the article of *S. Meyer* "Word Games" (DNA, Design and Intelligence) he finds out that the probability of achieving functional sequence of amino acids in several proteins is roughly 1 chance in 10^{65}. So the probability of life arising from chance is a very, very low probability – almost zero. An eminent astronomer Sir Fred Hoyle observed: "The current scenario of origin of life is about as likely as the assemblage of Boeing 747 by a tornado swirling through a junkyard." Subsequently, *Bill Gates* of Microsoft said: "DNA is like a computer program, but far, far more advanced than any software we ever created." This is just for one life; how much more for the billions or trillions of lives that inhabit the earth or the universe. And their numbers are increasing every minute not by arithmetical but instead by geometrical progression. These observations discredit the theory that life could have happened by accident as espoused by the Big Bang theorists. This theory was explained by a world famous British scientist, *Stephen Hawking* (whose intelligence is believed to be equal to that of *Albert Einstein*), who believes also that this is a possibility.

In 2001 another mathematician-philosopher, *Hari Kumar* came up with an article *"A Mathematical Analogy of God"* where he used an imaginary number line in relation to the real one. The real axis represents real matters, while the imaginary axis represents the soul, thoughts and the intangibles. They intersect at zero. The summation of positive and negative infinity is zero. His article, in my research so far, is the closest mathematical article written about God – an analogy of Him. It is interesting; you may like to read this article through the Internet.

Could World's Mysteries Be Explained?

V

*Mysteries are acts of God which are outside
manifestations of undiscovered hidden facts*

— *The Author*

From time immemorial, earlier philosophers (religious and political) and mathematicians tried to decipher the secrets of the universe. There are recurring phenomena which could not be explained up to modern times. To most people they are called mysteries which only the Creator could fathom. As the root causes of these mysteries are discovered, they basically follow the laws of physics and nature. Some are universal constants that could not be disproved like the *pi* (a transcendental number representing the ratio of a circle's circumference to its diameter), the speeds of sound and light, the gravitational force, the rotational and orbital movements of the planets, moons and stars and many more. These are discovered by serendipity, intuition or experimentations by the ever-searching human minds.

In early times, an eclipse was considered a mysterious phenomenon, which warned of a forthcoming calamity. People dreaded to watch the event, some submerged themselves in rivers and ponds, others kept their eyes fixed on the ground, pregnant women were warned and required to stay home, etc.

Through science, this event was discovered as a natural occurrence, which follows sets of pattern of planets' orbital and rotational movements in relation to one another. An eclipse occurs when the sun, moon and the earth are aligned, in which the moon is in between the two.

Another modern-day example is when a supersonic plane drops a bomb and hits a fast-moving target. To a layman, hitting the target at high speed is unbelievable if not amazing, but through the pilot's computer, it factored simply into account the Newton's gravitational force constant and Einstein's relativity equation.

These mysterious and amazing occurrences follow sets of patterns discovered by philosophers and scientists as laws of physics and universal constants. In scientific language, they describe the mathematical comprehensibility of the universe. As Einstein observed: "Miracles [or mysteries] are being constantly reinforced [discovered] as our own knowledge of science expands…"

These laws and constants are calibrated and fixed. Any change could cause domino effects or chain reactions that could alter the course of lives in the universe and may lead to a collapse of the world system.

Any of these changes could cause phenomena, which will be mysterious if not well understood in terms of the parameters of these universal constants and laws of physics. Suppose that the earth's gravity is reduced because of re-alignments of planets in our solar system, etc. How will these reductions, say 10% of gravity, affect us and those around us on earth? Some overweight people may joke that they are happy because they become lighter without resorting to diet or heavy exercise. An athlete, being lighter now, may say that he will immediately run in the 100-meter dash to set a new world record. These will just be the results in the short term. But the ultimate effect will be a great change in our entire environment and systems. The atmosphere, which is held by the earth's mass by gravitational pull, will partly disappear into space. With less atmosphere that serves as the earth's protective outside layer, the rays of the sun and stars will heat-up the earth. These will cause glaciers in the North and South Poles to melt and flow to the oceans, which will submerge lands. And in the evening, the earth will be exposed to the extreme universal coldness because of less protective atmosphere. These will lead to global heating and its sequel, global freezing much more catastrophic than the global warming and cooling our scientists are warning us about.

In the same way, change in the speed of light could have great effect on earth and the entire universe. An increase of speed by 5%, will heat-up the world; on the other hand, any decrease will trigger a cooling effect. In either way it will be catastrophic to the world's systems and will disturb the universal state of equilibrium.

Though these universal constants and laws of physics are fixed, some inherent changes in the universe occur through time. Somehow our universe gets stabilized too through the same time frame. The big question is: who continuously monitors, calibrates, and sets all of these for the universe and its inhabitants to survive?

Some of these well-known fundamental laws of physics are: General Relativity (Einstein's Equation), Quantum Mechanics (Schrodinger's Equations), Statistical Mechanics (Boltzmann's Equations), Electrodynamics (Maxwell's Equations) and others. Additionally, some of these already discovered universal constants are: speed of light at 670 million miles per hour, the speed of sound at 770 miles per hour, the Newton's gravitational force of the earth at 9.8 meter/sec², pi at 3.141 and others. Moreover, several scientific books explain the surprisingly mathematical comprehensibility of the universe. Some of these are the *"Cosmic Blueprint"*, *"Universal Constants in Physics"*, *"The Creation Hypothesis"*, etc.

Through time, more of universal constants and laws of physics will be discovered and they could explain the secrets of the world's mysteries. Suffice to say that they all point to one direction – that there is an intelligent designer behind all of these. And through this medium, could this intelligent designer's existence be proven too through mathematical equations?

The Mathematical Parameters

VI

It is the unquestioning acceptance of the already existing that prevents people from being creative.

– Anonymous

The first time I came across these mathematical parameters was when I was a senior student in high school. I never imagined that, as time passed by, these would be the tools to help me explain and prove the existence of a Creator – who created all things in the universe from the tiny grain of soil, thence to the rocks, thence to islands, to planets, to the universe, to the galaxies, to the "black holes" that all mysteriously exist around us. Mysteriously because we do not know how they were created but as you read through these mathematical parameters interacting against and with one another, they will explain the basic concept of creation of almost everything.

From one basic equation, the other two supporting equations were derived from it. It encapsulates the power of the Creator. This is the basic law that He uses in the exercise of His will and is the same one that every creation in the universe, whether animate or inanimate, follows.

The equation is based on the mathematical definition of *Infinity* represented by the standard symbol ∞. This idea started among Greek mathematicians—notably Archimedes—some 200 years before the birth of Christ. Since then, mathematicians and scientists have been and are using this formula in terms of numbers and figures only.

Now, 2,200 years later, let me decipher, correlate and interpret *Infinity* in terms of **divinity**. $\infty = N/n$ in which N is any member while n is a smaller number approaching but greater than zero. ∞ increases greatly as N increases or n decreases or both occurring simultaneously. This equation is universally accepted and used as a mathematical fact.

What then is the rationale why N could be designated as C which is creation and n could be a or alpha which is the origin or the seed of creation?

Through this ∞ equation, we will now proceed through the realm of *logic* in terms of the process of *deduction* or from an *established general statement of fact to specifics* coupled with mathematical transpositions.

Let us now interpret in ∞ terms of *divinity*.

Substituting, the *Infinity equation* in terms of **divinity** becomes $I=C/a$.

Through transposition, the basic equation is derived:

$$\boxed{C = I \times a}$$ - **Power to Create**

Where x and =: Mathematical symbols for multiplication and equality respectively

C : Is creation. Any matter that exists in the universe; it is represented by numerical values.

I : A symbol for *Infinity* or **Infinite Power** who is enormously great; expressed in terms of intensity of power with an acronym of *iop*.

44

a : Is alpha or beginning of creation. It is represented by lower numerical values, usually closer to zero or almost nothing. It is $a > 0$. *a* should be greater than zero.

Mathematically:

a multiplied by *I* equals to C. In layman's language: ***Infinity,*** *working on almost nothing that is a, creates C.* For simpler illustrations we will use smaller values. As will be shown in subsequent presentations, we will however use bigger values which reflect reality.

Example:
Let $I = 100$ *iop*
$a = .5$
Therefore by substitution in the formula:

Equation No. 1:
$$C = I \times a$$ **– Power to Create**
$$C = 100 \times .5$$
$$C = 50$$

C which is 50 is created from *a* with an intensity of power of 100 *iop*.

By transposition:
Equation No. 2:
$$a = C / I$$ **- Power to Punish/Destroy**

Example (using the same values):
Let $C = 50$
$I = 100$

Therefore by substitution in the formula:

$$a = C / I$$
$$= 50 / 100$$
$$a = .5$$

C at 50 is *reduced back* to *a* at .5, or one half. Then we go to the final equation, which is again done by transposition:

Equation No.3:

$$I = C / a$$ - **God Exists**

Example (using the same values):

Let C = 50

$a = .5$

Therefore by substitution in the formula:

$$I = C / a$$
$$= 50 / .5$$
$$I = 100 \ iop$$

With **I**'s intensity of power at 100 *iop*, *a* at .5 or one half could be *transformed* to 50 which could also be *transformed back* to the original *a* at .5 or one half.

These illustrations will enable you to review your high school mathematics. You will notice that by using the same or different values, the results are consistent. As we proceed to the following discussions at bigger values you could understand these simple algebraic transpositions and formulations which will make you appreciate the applications. While mathematics is an exact science, there might be some minor "fine tunings" in the final interpretation, but these are seemingly deliberate manifestations because only the Creator knows the exact interpretation.

Mathematical Equation No. 1

The Power to Create
VII

Einstein said: "God does not roll dice."
He was right: "God plays scrabble."

— Philip Gold

The definition of terms are reiterated here for the readers who need not flip back through the pages.

This formula is true:

Equation No.1: $\boxed{C = I \times a}$

where x and =: Mathematical symbols for multiplication and equality respectively

C: Is creation. Any matter that exist in the universe; it is represented by numerical numbers.

I : A symbol for **Infinity** or **Infinite Power** who is enormously great; expressed in terms of intensity of power with an acronym of *iop*.

a: Is alpha or beginning of creation. It is represented by smaller numerical values, usually closer to zero or almost nothing. It is *a >0. a* should be greater than zero.

SCENERY

Mathematically:

C equals I multiplies a. In layman's language, the illustration model shows that ***Infinity** works on **a** to create **C***. The italicized phrase in mathematical term is done by multiplication. (Refer to Illustration).

Example:
To save space, we will use exponents or numbers raised to the nth power.

Let I = 1 billion or 10^9 *iop*
a = .001 or $1/10^3$ or 10^{-3}

Substituting on the equation:

$C = I \times a$
$= 10^9 \times 10^{-3}$
$= 10^6$

$C = 1,000,000$ or 1 million

Another way of presentation is by direct substitution:

$C = I \times a$
$= 1,000,000,000 \times .001$
$= 1,000,000$

$C = 1$ million

I (10^9) *interacting with a* (.001) creates C that is equal to 1 million. That is the essence of the power to create. The numbers 10^9 or 1 billion represents God's power as He *creates* 10^6 or 1 million from almost nothing.

This power to create is illustrated in Genesis 1:1-2:25.

"The earth was empty, a formless mass cloaked in darkness. And the Spirit of God was hovering over its surface."

From here God created the day and night, waters and ground. "Let the land burst forth with every sort of grass and seed-bearing fruit. The seeds will then produce the kinds of plants and trees from which they came."

From the waters came fish and other life, and the skies filled with birds of every kind. Animals were created and ultimately, from Adam's rib He created Eve.

As could be observed from all of these, creation originated from something to almost nothing: "The earth was empty, a formless mass cloaked in darkness." Then subsequently came His famous advice: "Go forth and multiply." Mark 6:30-56

Jesus, together with his disciples, was preaching to a huge crowd. It was late afternoon and his disciples said: "This is a desolate place, and it is getting late. Send the crowds away so they can go to the nearby farms and villages and buy themselves some food."

But Jesus said, "You feed them."

"With what?" they asked. "It would take a small fortune to buy food for all this crowd!"

"How much food do you have?" He asked. "Go and find out."

They came back and reported, "We have five loaves of bread and two fish." Then Jesus told the crowd to sit down in groups on the green grass. So they sat in groups of fifty or a hundred.

Jesus took the five loaves and two fish, looked up toward heaven, and asked God's blessing on the food. Breaking the loaves into pieces, he kept giving the bread and fish to the disciples to give to the people. They all ate as much as they wanted, and they picked up twelve baskets of leftover bread and fish. Five thousand men had eaten from those original five loaves and two fish!

To illustrate the power to create, let us see how Jesus was able to feed 5,000 followers.

From the formula:
$$C = I \times a$$

1. For the bread:

Let $a = 5$ (the original loaves of bread)
$C = 2,500$ (the newly created loaves of bread; assuming two persons shared one loaf)

Substituting in the equation:
$$2,500 = I \times 5$$
$$I = 2,500 / 5$$
$$I = 500 \text{ } iop$$

2. For the fish:

Let $a = 2$ fish
$C = 5,000$ new fish (Assuming one fish per person)

Substituting in the equation:
$$5,000 = I \times 2$$
$$I = 5,000 / 2$$
$$I = 2,500 \text{ } iop$$

500 and 2,500 *iop* are the intensity of power that the **Infinite Power** (Creator) needed to create 2,500 loaves of bread and 5,000 fish. This exercise of power is flexible depending on the need. He could feed 100,000 followers and would need 10,000 *iop* and 50,000 *iop* to create bread and fish respectively.

As we perceive today, God's creation indeed had multiplied a million or billion times more. Out of these billions of creation on earth, let us take a look on this study as written by *Dr. Charles M. Crowe*[3] on the production of 100 bushels of corn on one acre of land:

> *"Man contributed the labour, God contributed a few things too: 4 million pounds of water, 6,800 pounds of oxygen, 5,200 pounds of carbon, 1,900 pounds of carbon dioxide, 160 pounds of nitrogen, 125 pounds of potassium, 40 pounds of phosphorous, 75 pounds of yellow sulphur, 50 pounds of magnesium, 50 pounds of calcium, two pounds of iron, and small amounts of iodine, zinc, copper and other things – and they're all inside 100 bushels of corn! Who made it?"*

From several hundred corn seeds, one hundred bushels of corn nourished with all these elements in two months from just a small parcel of earth is one of the many simple wonders of His power of creation.

Illustration

Power to Create

$$C = I \times a$$

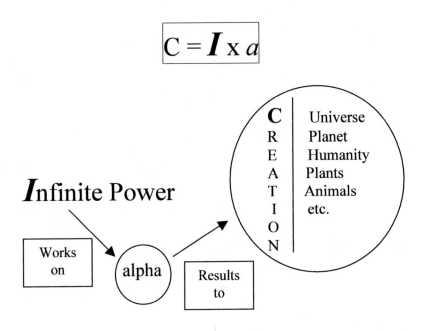

"The earth was empty, a formless mass cloaked in darkness." From there God created everything

- Genesis 1:2

Afterthoughts

Mathematical Equation No. 2

The Power to Punish
VIII

Let him who sins when drunk
be punished when sober.

– Legal Maxim

Transposing from equation No.1, which is true, therefore, this formula is also true:

Equation No.2: $\boxed{a = C / I}$

Mathematically:

    a equals C divided by I. In layman's words, the illustration model shows that a matter is *"cut into pieces"* by the **Infinite Power I** that *results to* almost nothing. (Refer to Illustration).

Example:

    The values are the same as in the previous illustration.

$$Let\ C = 10^6\ (one\ million)$$
$$I = 10^9\ (one\ billion)\ iop$$

Substituting these in the equation:

$$\boxed{a = C / I}$$
$$= 10^6/10^9$$
$$= 10^6 / 10^6 \times 10^3 = 1 / 10^3$$
$$\boxed{a = .001}$$

SCENERY

Another way of presentation is by direct substitution:

$$a = C / I$$
$$= 1,000,000 / 1,000,000,000$$
$$= 1 / 1,000$$
$$a = .001$$

I (10^9) *dividing* C (10^6) *makes the result* 1/1000 or .001 which is almost nothing. This is, in essence, the Power to Punish or Destroy. It shows how matters are reduced to almost nothing when God uses graduated intensity of power to punish the nonbelievers or those who defy him.   He gives warnings first through increasing severity of His punishments.

His exercise of power is well exemplified in Exodus.

The Lord said to Moses, "Go to the Pharaoh once again and tell him, this is what the Lord says, 'Let my people go, so they can worship me'.   If he refuses then listen to this carefully..."

When the Pharaoh refused to listen to the Lord, Moses raised his staff and hit the Nile River. The river turned into blood and eventually all the fishes died. Blood was everywhere and devastated Egypt.

In spite of this, the Pharaoh remained stubborn. The Lord meted him out more punishments.   He sent a deadly plague that destroyed the livestock of Egypt but spared Israel.

But the last straw came when God declared that all first-born sons and first-born male animals shall be killed.   And this was done to include the first-born son of the Pharaoh.

Finally, the Pharaoh gave up and told Moses: "Leave us," he cried.   "Go away, all of you!   Go and serve the Lord as you have requested."

There were numerous punishments and destructions that the Lord inflicted in the form of miracles. His power reduces anything and anyone to almost nothingness – "from dust you came, to dust you shall return." (Genesis 3:19)

This becomes part of the religious rite when ashes are put in the sign of the cross upon the foreheads of the faithful. It reminds that dust symbolizes the beginning and end of living creation; that birth and death are inevitable partners in life. Dust is an important link of creation.

In 2002, Whole Earth published an article, the "Secret Life of Dust"[4] which mentions the history of dust. Can dust submerge land? Can it move mountains? We will say that this is impossible.

Let us analyze.

In the North Pole, the snow reflects the heat of the sun by 80%. But if there is a patch of dust somewhere on it, the heat is absorbed and little by little the snow melts. As the patch of dirt expands and grows due to molding, chemical decomposition and environmental pollution, the snow melts on larger scale. And with this process continuing through millions of years, more snow melts and flows into rivers and oceans thereby submerging land. As more water flows inland, the foundations of mountains are weakened, the rocks and soil turned into dust thence to mud. We heard of islands that disappeared and mountains that crumbled to their foundations.

The article also mentions that a puff of cigarette contains some four billion particles of dust. From the dust we will try to measure our Creator's intensity of power when He punishes His creations by transforming them back to dust.

The world today has around 2.4 billion nonbelievers and 4 billion believers. Around 37 percent of His human creations does not believe on Him. He has given them sufficient warnings of His Second Coming. How powerful is He?

Let us measure His power from the equation $a = C/I$.

C = 2.4 billion nonbelievers

a = The particle of dust that He could transform each nonbeliever into. This dust could be as minute at 1×10^{-10}.

Substituting in the equation, it appears like this:

$1 \times 10^{-10} = 2.4 \times 10^{9} / I$

$I = 2.4 \times 10^{9} / 1 \times 10^{-10}$

$= 2.4 \times 10^{19}$

$I = 24{,}000{,}000{,}000{,}000{,}000{,}000$ *iop*

This is His intensity of power that will bear upon the nonbelievers. His might is beyond human comprehension and description. It is 24 billion billion *iop*! How enormous is this? In Part VII - Power to Create, God used 500 *iop* in creating 2,500 loaves of bread from 5 loaves. 24 billion billion *iop* is 5×10^{17} times more powerful. In a layman's language, that is 500 billion million times more.

How about a nonbeliever's power to counter this? Or say, any human for that matter. Is he that powerful enough? Let us measure it through the same equation. Since he has no ability on his own to naturally create something from anything, his creativity is therefore zero. A nonbeliever's intensity of power is calculated this way by substituting $C = 0$ in the equation:

$a = C/I$

$a = 0/I$

$I = 0/a$

$I = 0$ *iop*

It is mathematically clear that a nonbeliever or for that matter, all the 2.4 billion nonbelievers in this world have a combined intensity of power equals to zero!

How are they compared to their Creator? Nothing!!

But our Creator still faithfully watches over them, waits for them to come to His fold. He expects them to re-evaluate themselves and they will be welcomed should they acknowledge Him. Anytime. He still cares for them. Why wait?

Luke 21:5-28

Some of his disciples began talking about the beautiful stonework of the Temple and the memorial decorations on the walls. But Jesus said, "The time is coming when all these things will be completely demolished that not one stone will be left on top of another. Nations and kingdoms will proclaim war against each other. There will be great earthquakes, and there will be famines and epidemics in many lands, and there will be terrifying things and great miraculous signs in the heavens.

"And there will be strange events in the skies – signs in the sun, moon, and stars. And down here on earth, the nations will be in turmoil, perplexed by the roaring seas and strange tides. The courage of many people will falter because of the fearful fate they see coming upon the earth, because the stability of the very heavens will be broken up. Then everyone will see the Son of Man arrives on the clouds with power and great glory."

After so many warnings and stubborn defiance of men, the Creator will finally use all His might. Shall they go back to almost nothingness again? As shown mathematically, it is possible and could happen under His power to punish or destroy. Realistically, He could do it.

Illustration

Power to Punish / Destroy

$$a = C / I$$

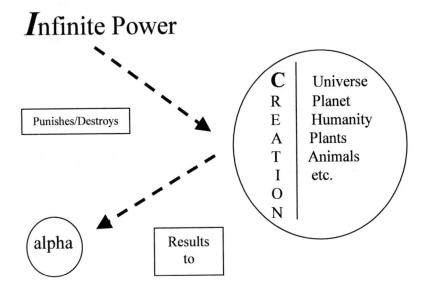

Infinite Power

Punishes/Destroys

C
R
E
A
T
I
O
N

Universe
Planet
Humanity
Plants
Animals
etc.

alpha

Results
to

"From dust you cometh, to dust you returneth."

- Genesis 3:19

Afterthoughts

Mathematical Equation No. 3

God Exists
IX

*All I have seen teaches me to trust the Creator
for all I have not seen.*

— *Ralph Waldo Emerson*

Transposing from equations No.1 and/or No.2, which are true, this next formula is therefore true. Moreover, this is the revisited and "reincarnated" Archimedes ∞ equation.

Equation No.3: $\boxed{I = C / a}$

Mathematically:

I equals C *divided by a.* In other words, a matter or a number that is divided by a very small number *results to* an enormous amount that is *I.*

The equation is represented by a graphic illustration model which shows that the ***Infinite Power*** could *"elevate"* or *work on **a*** to become ***C;*** or could *"put down"* or *revert C back* to its origin ***a.*** (Refer to Illustration).

The values are the same as in the two previous illustrations.

$$\text{Let } C = 10^6$$
$$a = .001$$

SCENERY

Substituting in the equation:

$$I = C / a$$
$$= 10^6 / .001$$
$$= 10^6 / 10^{-3}$$
$$= 10^6 \times 10^3$$
$$I = 10^9 \text{ or } 1 \text{ billion } iop$$

Or another way of presentation is by direct substitution:

$$I = 1,000,000 / .001$$
$$= 1,000,000 \times 1,000$$
$$= 1,000,000,000$$
$$I = 1 \text{ billion } iop$$

C (10^6) *divided by* a (.001) *results to* an enormously great I which is 10^9.

This equation could also be explained through this procedure. A more idealistic value of a is reached or attained as its value moves closer to zero ($a \rightarrow 0$) making the value of I to increase. Say $1/1,000 = a$ (which is also equal to .001). For example, if one apple is divided by a thousand people, the share of each person is almost nothing.

By substitutions and transposition on the formula:

$$I = C / a$$
$$= C / 1 / 1,000 = C \times 1,000 / 1$$
$$I = C \times 1000$$

This final equation $I = C \times 1,000$ will then be exactly the same as in the previous illustration:

$$10^6 \times 10^3 = 10^9$$

C could be by the billions (10^9), trillions (10^{12}) or more and a could be by the thousandths, i.e. (10^{-3}) or less which will result to a very enormous I indeed.

From this equation we can draw a mental picture: as more people share this one apple, the greater is the value of *Infinity*.

In the formula:

$I = C \times 10^3$

Then it may be:

$C \times 10^7$ or $C \times 10^8$ resulting to much bigger I as shown in this example:

$= 10^6 \times 10^8$

$I = 10^{14}$!

I is the personification or representation of God. His power rests upon all of humanity so great in number, hopefully to be all united under His umbrella when everyone shares the belief that He is that one and only Creator.

May I emphasize that when a becomes smaller (like more people are sharing one apple or one belief), it has a bigger "multiplier" effect and results to a much greater value of *Infinity*.

As shown in the calculation of His Power to Punish or Destroy in Part VIII, I wish to present here the total intensity of power our Creator exercises and is exercising in creating humans and convincing them to believe Him.

In the equation: $I = C/a$

$C = 6.4$ billion is the total world population as of this year.

$a = 1 \times 10^{-10}$. The particle of dust that a human could be transformed back to its origin with value of almost zero.

66

Substituting in the equation:

$I = C/a$

$=6.4 \text{ billion } /1\text{x}10^{-10}=6.4\text{x}10^{9}/1\text{x}10^{-10}$

$=6.4\text{x}10^{19}$

$= 64,000,000,000,000,000,000$ *iop*

$I = 64$ billion billion *iop*

This is the total intensity of power our Creator has over human creation alone. With the trillions of other creations, His power is boundless. It's *Infinity*.

As the number of His creations increases through time, His intensity of power also increases indefinitely in the same proportion. Could you mentally picture how great and powerful He is?

Summarizing, here again are the three equations:

Equation No. 1: $C = I$ x a – Power to Create

Equation No. 2: $a = C / I$ – Power to Punish

Equation No. 3: $I = C / a$ – God Exists

Equations No. 1 and 2 lay the foundation for the final equation showing that God exists. In mathematics, since equation No.1 (Power to Create) is true, thence equation No.2 (Power to Punish), which is derived from No.1, is also true, and therefore the final equation No.3 (God Exists), which is derived from both equations 1 and 2, must be true. Moreover, this equation No. 3 is the original *Infinity* or ∞ equation.

Through mathematics, we just proved that all the equations are true starting from *I* thence to *C* to *a*. Or this could be also done and proven through the reverse way: from *a* to *C* to *I*.

Additionally, through *logic* it also proved the correctness of the equations or statements through the process of *deduction* (from *general statement of fact to specifics*). However, this could also be proven through the reverse process of *induction* which is from *specifics to general statement.*

Moreover, each of the mathematical equation fits into each respective illustration model which expresses in simple graphic terms the meaning of the Creator's power.

Interestingly, mathematics, logic, and these graphic illustration models *interweave with one another* to become ONE. Significantly, this ONE very well conforms with theology (Scriptures) to prove an incontestable and unquestionable truth – that there is an *Infinite Power I* who is God.

His existence is manifested and reinforced by His omnipotence in terms of His creation as explained in Genesis and punishments as revealed in the Revelations and all of these throughout the Scriptures.

His powers are encapsulated in the Cycle of Creation. All of these settle down to an undeniable and living truth – that God exists.

Illustration

God Exists

$$I = C / a$$

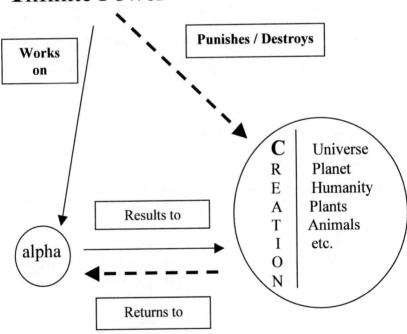

God's Cycle of Creation

"I am the Alpha and the Omega . . .
I am the All-Powerful"

- Revelations 1:8

Afterthoughts

Conclusion

X

*When God conceived the world, that was poetry. He
formed it and that was sculpture. He colored it and that
was painting. He peopled it with living beings and that
was grand, eternal, divine drama*

- David Belasco

As shown and explained under His power to
create and to punish, then ultimately to the equation that
God exists, we realize how enormous are His intensities
of power over all creation. Under the power to create, God
needed 500 *iop* (intensity of power) to feed some 5,000
followers from the original five loaves of bread. He has
under His power some 24 billion billion (24×10^{18}) *iop* to
punish the 2.4 billion nonbelievers on earth. And to keep and
care for the 6.4 billions people of the world, He utilizes some
64 billion billion (64×10^{18}) *iop*. These divine equations
define the identity and dimensions of the Creator that
could only be described in the best superlatives of
goodness and greatness.

The final equation, $I = C / a$ is significant
because it emanated and was derived from His creativity
(power to create) and strength (power to punish).

Though these equations are expressed in cold and
lifeless figures, they nevertheless represent and mirror
the natural laws that govern the existence of animate
and inanimate creation in the universe. Through the
interactions of the parameters in these equations we see,
feel and understand through our eyes and minds, that in

reality God is around us. Though He is with us – in the past, present and future– He is a part of us inasmuch as we are a part of Him. For us to exist, we have to be a part of Him to feel his enormous power. He loves us regardless of our gender, race, faith or whatever differences we have with one another.

These equations are the first of their kind to show in mathematical equations that God really exists. They could serve as bases for further study to reduce whatever imperfections they may have. I may not be perfect and I leave it to God to fill in these gaps. My aim is simply to inform the whole of humanity – the believers and nonbelievers alike – that we are all living on a common condition: God created us and it behooves us to look up to Him with gratitude for our existence. The fact that most things are going well in our planet, in our universe and ultimately in ourselves proves that God's powers are radiating to and within us.

Many scientists, mathematicians, intellectuals, etc., oftentimes find it hard to believe that there is a God. They search for clues or answers in concrete terms but many have failed.

To the believers, they are very fortunate enough to understand the existence of God. May their knowledge of these equations further reinforce their faith. To the nonbelievers, please review these mathematical equations and ask yourselves: "Are these not the same simple equations that we use as tools in calculating scientific researches in physics, engineering, computer science, aeronautics, space explorations, thermodynamics, and the like?" Surely they are. You are doing these things right under your very eyes; you are writing these equations with your fingers; you are figuring them out in your minds. God created you but it's quite paradoxical that you are looking too far in your quest for the answer. The answer is there – it's within you; your existence yourself as a distinctive human. At times, your failure to see His existence is just your mindset.

The facts that we are all individualized humans and that all other creatures and creation in our midst have distinctive differentiations from each other are some of the simple wonders of the Creator. Through time, He will create more. However, some of those that may not conform to His laws of nature will have to perish, as it is His way of punishing and destroying things that cause imbalance in our system. This is God's "check and balance" to enable His creation to exist for billions of years or probably up to eternity. This is the Cycle of Creation. Dinosaurs that existed millions of years ago became extinct because under the natural law of "survival of the fittest," they could not have survived indeed through modern times; newer species of animals replaced them and many still exist to these times.

Francis Bacon (1561-1626), an English philosopher, statesman, and one of the pioneers of modern scientific knowledge, wrote: "There are two books laid before us to study, to prevent our falling into error: First, the volumes of the Scriptures which reveal the will of God; then the volumes of Creatures which express His power." Therefore, this mathematical equation ($I = C / a$) reconciled, intertwined and married these two – the Scriptures and the Creatures.

By and large, these creations and their ways of life are manifested and explained in these divine equations that prove that there is definitely a Creator, who designs and creates all of these; and is still continuously doing them; indeed **God exists!**

These Divine Equations' Impact on Major Theories and Religions

XI

1. Theory of Evolution:

Charles Darwin theorized that all living things originated from a single ancestor through processes of natural selection of minor variations or modifications and mutation over a long period of time. Some examples are the common depiction that man came from the primitive apes and that a complex-cell creature originated from a single – cell organism.

In this divine equation: $C = I \times a$ where, C stands for creation and a for alpha or beginning, it is important to note that a and C must have the same unit of measure or for that matter, the same species. Mathematically, the equation collapses when a and C have different units. If a is a man then the outcome C should be men; or if a is an ape, then C should be apes. In like manner that if a is an apple seed, then C should be an apple tree, ad infinitum. It could not be in any other way.

Moreover, in the living memory of mankind, no one yet had noticed any slight variation or change (through natural selection or mutation) in the appearance of domesticated or wild apes. No ape yet so far had turned to resemble close to a man.

However, the mathematical equation above is in conformity or in agreement with Genesis specifically the following which state:

Verse 11-". . . Every seed will produce more of its own kind of plant. And it happened . . . "

Verse 21- ". . . And each bird produces more of its own kind . . ."

Verse 24 – ". . .And each animal produces more of its own kind . . ."

Verse 27- "So God created human beings in his image . . ."

Upon creating them as distinct species, He gave them His benediction: "Go forth and multiply."

This divine equation (DE) through mathematics, logic, graphic illustration models, and reinforced with theology and empirical observations refutes the Evolution Theory.

2. Intelligent Design (ID)

Generally, believers know *who* created the universe. Presently , there comes the pursuit of a field in science on *how* was the universe created. This is within the realm of Intelligent Design. It injects scientific investigations on *how* the universe exists to include its animate and inanimate objects; that they all follow sets of physical laws and universal constants that govern the state of the whole world and the galaxies. The supporters of this theory have found out that the probability is almost zero for a human being to originate from one single-cell organism, even if it takes 100 billion years of natural selection and mutation processes. Generally, the ID refutes the evolutionists. It also dismisses the idea that life could evolve through time from an explosion as spoused by the Big Bang theorists. The ID's primary factor is an intelligent designer *who* does all of these and shows *how.* He is none other than the Creator.

As far as the divine equations (DE) as presented here, they are in conformity with all aspects of the ID. DE being founded also on mathematics, follow the mainstream of methodology, logic and findings of the ID.

3. The Big Bang Theory

As early as 1914 scientists theorized that some galaxies from time immemorial moved away at great speeds that later ushered in the Big Bang Theory. The explosion caused the creation of the universe. This made world-famous physicist Stephen Hawking and co-theorists believe that the universe started from nothing; that there was nothing at all before the explosion: a "day without yesterday". It is also their contention that there is no relevance for a creator because everything was caused alone by the "burst of fireworks" from a super-hot point in time, some 15 billion years ago.

As pointed out in my earlier presentation, the probability of a single-cell life occurring due to that explosion is 1 to 10^{65} or more; it's almost zero. So, could more complex living creatures, like man, originate from that accident? It's more impossible.

In the divine equation: $I = C/a$, a or $alpha$ by definition could not be zero. It should be something or any amount greater than zero. If a is nothing as stated by the Bing Bang theorists, then the divine equations would not work at all because any number or amount divided by zero is mathematically undefined and not permissible.

Genesis 1:2 states: ". . . The earth was empty, a formless mass cloaked in darkness . .." From there God created everything. What is noteworthy in this verse is the word <u>mass</u>. Dictionary defines <u>mass</u> as a coherent body of matter having no definite shape but relatively large in size. In short, a is something else but not nothing!

Even if we go back before the "beginning" as stated in Genesis 1:1, modern scientist have theorized that the universe was expanding since 15 billion years ago. This was also the findings of Albert Einstein as stated in his General Theory of Relativity. If we travel back through space and time, it may show that the world was a very compact and enormous matter at very high temperature that may have instantaneously exploded. In short, before the explosion, there was already something that existed, most likely a huge solid mass. But not nothing at all. Who created this?

John 1;1-3 states: "Before the world began, there was the Word. The Word was with God and the Word was God.

He was with God in the beginning. All things were made through him. Nothing was made without Him . . ."

The Creator was not just there thousand of years before the 2,500 years of recorded history of the Scriptures but long before an explosion (if there was) or before the "beginning" – 15 billion years, or could it be more?

Moreover, Colossians 1:17 states: "And He is before all things, and in Him all things hold together."

He reigns from everlasting to everlasting.

Therefore, this divine equation through mathematics reinforced by logic, graphic illustration models combined with theology and latest scientific studies refutes the explosion theory.

4. World Religions

Wernher von Braun (1912-1977), one of the world's top space scientist who later became head of NASA once said: "An outlook through this peephole (that manned space flight had opened) at the vast mysteries of the universe should only confirm our belief in the certainty of the Creator. I find it as difficult to understand a scientist who does not acknowledge the presence of a superior rationality behind the existence of the universe as it is to comprehend a theologian who would deny the advances of science."

Science and religion are congruent, practical, and effective partners in discovering more the *who* and *how* of the universe – *who* really is the Creator and *how* do phenomena occur as wondrous and at times miraculous. Once we comprehend and understand these, the more we appreciate the enormity of His greatness and power and the secrets of the universe.

Being humans, there are hundreds if not thousands of occurrences that escape our observations. We only react to forebodings when the ill effects are already manifested in our midst and the process becomes irreversible. This is the case of *global warming* which in the long run is a threat to human existence on earth.

Gaze at the skies on starry nights and wonder at the great expanse of the Creator's intelligence, creativity, presence and power. Like an astronaut, let's go beyond the surface of the earth, imaginatively; look and do things around us from different perspectives and not on our usual ways.

In this era of information superhighway , let us join hands in the pursuit of scientific researches while enhancing our spiritual enlightenment as well.

A friend who is a corporate manager shyly confided to me that whenever he encounters problems requiring computer know-hows, he relies on his 12-year old son to figure them out.

Like him, must it be that we resist change and dwell too long on our comfort zones year in year out, that new knowledge and technology are just passing us by? The truism -- Innovate or Stagnate -- is just an appropriate reminder for us.

While many nonbelievers, evolutionists, Big Bang theorists, Intelligent Design proponents, etc. are progressing in terms of acquiring and utilizing knowledge and technology, mustn't we do the same to understand more the Creator and comprehend better the wonders of His phenomena? And when we make discoveries, let's announce them proudly to the world to make everyone more appreciative of the power of a Creator whose intelligence and creativity are beyond the combined brainpower of the 6.4 billion humans on earth.

These divine equations may just be one of them. There will be more to be discovered if ever we will think and act along this way. We would not lose anything, but humanity will instead gain much more. Corollarily, I personally believe that the Creator likes to communicate with us through this rational way too.

Moreover, if you are believers based on faith, isn't it your obligation as well to contribute your share of the Divine Commission—to pursue your divine mission of spreading His gospel to everyone including the nonbelievers, agnostics, atheists and the like? Could these divine equations be of help? Greatly.

Finally, it is my hope that we earnestly join in His bandwagon of unraveling more about Him through both faith and science as we travel beyond human horizon.

SCENERY

Afterthoughts

Reflections

XII

The difference between ordinary
and extraordinary is that little extra.

– Easter Morning Inspirations

Have you ever wondered how the billions of animate and inanimate objects in this world were created? As you have read in the previous part of this book, it is amazing how a bushel of corn was created – to make it edible to further support the ecosystem of the earth. God created cycles for the earth and its inhabitants so that they could go on through billions of years. It is noteworthy to look into this cycle of the fauna (animal) kingdom: men eat animals, animals eat smaller animals, smaller animals eat insects, insects eat bacteria, bacteria eat viruses and viruses eat men.... And the same is true with the flora (plant) kingdom: big trees shade and feed (as fertilizer) on small trees, small trees feed on smaller trees, smaller trees feed on grass (weeds, vines and ferns) and grass feeds on trees....

Are these cycles caused by accident? By evolution? Hardly.

Have you ever experienced a small bee buzzing near your face? It could fly horizontally or vertically, could walk or crawl upward and downward, could abruptly change directions faster than the wink of an eye, could protect itself with its painful sting, could pollinate plants' flowers so that they may bear fruits, could collect honey for the queen bee and her offspring.

Most fascinating is its life, its ability to breathe, fight and survive. This is an amazing creature, which cannot be duplicated by accident or by evolution, not even by robotic specialists. Indeed, there is an intelligent designer[5].

When a child was asked how was the earth created, she replied – "The earth was created for six days using only one hand."

"Why only one hand?"

"Because the Bible says that Jesus was in God's right arm."

On the other hand, God has ways of "punishing" some people. *Howard Jarvis[6] relates this:*

"A [shrewd] politician was speaking with God about values and he asked Him, 'What is a minute worth in heaven?'

God replied, 'A billion years.'

Then he asked God, 'What is a penny worth in heaven?'

God replied, 'A billion dollars.'

[Thinking that is a great opportunity to raise campaign funds], the politician then asked, 'God, could you give me a penny?'

And God said, 'Of course my son, I'll give you; wait a minute'".

God has a way of healing us. That is why He gave only to humans the ability to smile and laugh. From this we discover that indeed "laughter is the best medicine" that He shares with us, though I have not heard about His son Jesus healing through laughter.

As I was writing this, I received a timely e-mail from a friend. We exerted efforts to trace the origin but we failed because it might have passed through so many hands already. It might be nice to share this with you because it could uplift your spirits.

"From a strictly mathematical viewpoint:

What equals 100%?

What does it mean to give MORE than 100%?

Ever wonder about those people who say they are giving more than 100%?

We have all been in situations where in someone wants you to give over 100%. What equals 100% in life?

How about achieving 101%?

Here's a little "mathematical formula" that might help you answer these questions:

If:

A B C D E F G H I J K L M N O P Q R S T U V W X Y Z

are represented as:

1 2 3 4 5 6 7 8 9 10 11 12 13 14 15 16
17 18 19 20 21 22 23 24 25 26

Then:

$\underline{K - N - O - W - L - E - D - G - E}$

11+14+15+23+12+5+4+7+5=96%

and

$\underline{H - A - R - D - W - O - R - K}$

8+1+18+4+23+15+18+11=98%

But,

$\underline{A - T - T - I - T - U - D - E}$

1+20+20+9+20+21+4+5=100%

AND, look how far the love of God will take you

$\underline{L - O - V - E - O - F - G - O - D}$

12+15+22+5+15+6+7+15+4=101%

*Therefore, one can conclude with mathematical certainty that while **Knowledge** and **Hard work** will get* *you close, and **Attitude** will get you there, it's the **Love of God** that will put you over the top!"*

After reading through these mathematical proofs, you might be enamored by using mathematics to help you solve some problems in life or at least overcome some of them. Here is the story of a dedicated mathematician who asked God:

"Lord, are there mathematical symposia in Heaven?"

The Lord replied: "Well, there are good news and exciting news."

"God tell me first the good news."

"The good news is there are conferences in Heaven."

"Great! Now what is the exciting news?"

God replied: "Next week, the scheduled presenter is you!"

I do not mean to disrupt or lessen your faith in God. On the contrary it is my hope to merely reinforce it. As for the nonbelievers it is now a good chance to rediscover yourselves in relation to the Creator through this book.

But why are many religious authorities sounding notes of alarm with the showing of the movie "The DaVinci Code," which they perceive as blasphemous? Are they apprehensive that this will cause cracks in their faith? But if believers know God not only based on faith but also through concrete and rational facts, their relationship with God could withstand any storm that shall pass by.

During my early college years, I remember our professor explained to us some intricate applications of a mathematical equation. We could hardly understand it. From this scenario, we could differentiate between "fact" and "faith."

That he was in front of us and explained the lesson are "facts." That we listened and tried to understand him is "faith." Facts are physical representation of an event while faith is a subjective measure of belief, comprehension or learning from such.

That day after our professor explained the lesson, he gave us a spot quiz.

The following meeting, he looked unhappy. "The result of the test is unsatisfactory," he said. "This is a significant equation that I wouldn't want you to miss. Let's go through the basic, the derivation and its applications again."

Our professor was patient as we went through the step-by-step process. Eventually, we learned to appreciate the equation. Decades had passed and we still know it by heart – the Law of Relativity by Albert Einstein. The moral of the story is that reinforcing faith with the actual learning and going through a rational and/or mathematical process not only increases perception and comprehension but also sustains retention.

As you search through the Internet under the subject "Mathematical Proofs that God Exists" there are so many articles written about it. Some articles are serious, others are entertaining and the rest are just plain funny. Every writer seems to be at wit's end attempting to decipher the truth of His existence. Some are of few pages while others are in few sentences only. What is interesting is this article written by Mr. Ronnie Bryan, a graduate of the Massachusetts Institute of Technology (MIT) with a degree in Brain and Cognitive Science. Whatever value it could contribute to our discussion, I leave it to the readers to evaluate its worth. Months ago, I sent an e-mail to Mr. Bryan inquiring further on this discovery. I feel very appreciative that we have the same desire to decipher our Creator or God. May Mr. Bryan's tribe increase and God is pleased to bless him.

Mr. Bryan uses the value of *pi*, which is the ratio of the earth's or circle's circumference to its diameter. With the use of a special calculator, he found out the value of *pi* with the following sequence of numbers.

pi=3.1415...85121215208919919715419165111914785 18591139318512054208

He took each number, starting with 8, correspondingly to its placement in the English alphabet:

a b c d e f g h I j k l m n o p q r s t u v w x y z
1 2 3 4 5 6 7 8 9 10 11 12 13 14 15 16 17 18 19 20 21 22 23 24 25 26

The result is:

heababaeb0hiaiiaigaedaiafeaaaiadgheaheiaacicaheab0 edb0hebaadibbea

Since there is no zero (0) in the alphabet, he takes zero to mean either 10 or 20 and taking zero as either 1 or 2 the message shows:

hellothisisgodspeakinghereiamicreatedtheuniverse

Since there are no punctuations in the alphabet, Mr. Bryan said that it could either be:

Hello. This is God speaking. Here I am. I created the universe.

or

Hello this is God speaking here. I AM. I created the universe.

Amazing isn't it? You may try it yourself.

After reading the initial manuscript of this book, Med Justiniano, a retired colonel and ex-chaplain of the Veterans of Foreign Wars Guam, USA observes:

"This is very interesting and creative. It is soul searching. These divine equations are mind-openers for the four billion believers especially for the more than two billion nonbelievers worldwide. This new insight elevates further our belief in our Creator, our God – religion with faith reinforced with intellectualism."

It is my hope that God will make more revelations about these equations because as of now, they are beyond my concept or imagination as a human. His intelligence is far greater than the combined brainpower of the six billion plus humans on earth.

Sometime in the middle part of February 2007, I joined a science class in a presentation about the universe at the University of Guam Planetarium. While waiting for the attendees at the Science Building, I read some posted reading materials about the universe. There was the arrangement of the earth in relation to other planets vis-à-vis their distances from the sun. It was a pleasant surprise that I easily memorized the arrangement in a matter of several seconds, which I never could have memorized in my entire student life ... from elementary to college years: that the arrangement of planets could easily be remembered through this mnemonic lines: "My very eager mother just serves us noodles."

The first letter of each word stands respectively for: Mercury, Venus, Earth, Mars, Jupiter, Saturn, Uranus and Neptune. What happened to Pluto? It is the smallest and the farthest from the sun. Recently, it was demoted from the status of planet; while before it was the "tail of the lion", it is now the "head of the cat", the "king" in its own group of smaller celestial bodies in its area.

During the show, the presenter explained in the projection room the planets, stars and the enormous span of the galaxies, that all of these celestial bodies follow sets of laws in their rotational and orbital movements that are unaltered through billions of years of existence, among others.

After some questions were asked and were satisfactorily answered, I asked a question which momentarily caused the presenter to pause. My question: With all of these enormous grandeur and mysteries of the universe, is there a great designer?

And with all frankness, she shrugged her shoulders and replied: "I don't know." I understand why she answered this way because no human yet had actually discovered scientifically the answer to my question.

As I was leaving the projection room, I asked myself this same question. It is very impossible that there is no designer to harmonize all of these planets and stars, their movements in space at thousands of miles per hour, their great solid mass continuously orbiting yet not colliding against one another. And there are thousands or millions of them in space! I thought that on earth, while driving a vehicle on our roads, it could collide with another at any moment; and these two vehicles are manned by two intelligent humans. On the other hand, these spherical "pilot-less" or "unmanned" celestial bodies many measuring thousand of miles in diameter do not collide against each other through billions of years of continuous motion. A collision of planets, if it occurs, will be catastrophic of unimaginable proportion.

While driving back home, I subconsciously was singing an old song. Then I realized that this moving excerpt is exactly the answer to my question. The Creator in His way categorically answered it:

"Oh Lord my God
When I in awesome wonder
Consider all the worlds thy hands have made
I see the stars, I hear the rolling thunder,
Thy power throughout the universe displayed."

God must be bigger and greater than the universe. When anyone (out of the 6 billion plus humans) prays, He listens. As the Scripture in Jeremiah 33:3 says, "Call to Me, I will answer you, and show you great and mighty things, which you do not know".

This further reminded me of a story, *"Mystery of the Peanut,"* by *Dr. Purnell Bailey*[7] about *George Washington Carver* (1864 –1943), a very famous US educator, innovator and scientist who was born in Missouri, USA. Take note that the years of his birth and death are inconsequential. What is important is what happened in his "—" (the dash between the years):

"He asked the Lord, "Lord, what is the universe made for?"

And God answered, "George, the universe is too big for you to understand. Suppose you just let me take care of the universe."

Then he humbly asked, "Lord, if the universe is too big for me to understand, how about the peanut?"

Then God answered him. "Now, George, you have something your size. You can understand a peanut, so I will help you."

So Dr. Carver left the universe to God's care and discovered the <u>might</u> of the little peanut. And from it he developed more than 200 useful products. And not once did he complain that God had withheld the deeper secrets from him."

So let's leave the universe to God and humble ourselves as just peanuts. After all, He is the Great Organizer and Designer – whose acronym is **G.O.D.**

SCENERY

Afterthoughts

Intricate Ways of His Intentions

XIII

Who can measure the enigma of the Creator's dimensions and predict His intentions? Only one. Himself... God.

- *The Author*

Power to Punish and to Love

At times God seems to punish us but His ultimate desire is for us to follow His good ways and to feel His immense love. In my younger days, my older brother related the experience of his childhood friend, Lester Cruz. He was an atheist.

One day Lester went to his farm. He was viewing the beautiful mountain scenes when he accidentally stepped on a cobra. He panicked as the snake lunged its ugly head to his leg. Good, he was able to avoid the deadly thrust. He ran away as fast as he could. But unfortunately he fell from the cliff and plunged down below. But luckily this time, he fell on a thick foliage of a tree growing by the side of the ravine. He looked down as his eyes seemed to pop out: it was a 100–foot deep ravine. Down below was a dried-up river lined up with boulders of rocks. He was, for the moment, glad that he did not plunge directly to his painful death.

Recovering from the shock of almost being bitten by a cobra and now sitting on one of the branches of a tree that was hanging by the cliff, he realized that he had no way out for a good escape.

For almost a whole day he kept on shouting for help until he lost his voice and his strength. The whole night he sat wide-awake crying that he must not give up as he would surely plunge to his death. He didn't know what to do.

On the second day, thirsty and hungry, he was trying to stop words which his heart wanted to shout out. He just subdued those words asking for God's help; his conscious mind refused to give in.

On the third day, he was already so weak and delirious. He knew that anytime he would fall. This time his mind gave up. He summoned all his strength and shouted: "God forgive me... Please help me!"

He waited for a moment. Silence. He continued to cry and whispered words of atonement for his sins, his great disobedience and disbelief in God.

Then in the middle of the night a storm approached. There was continuous heavy downpour and stormy, chilling winds. He was surviving from the leaves that he ate and the water from the morning dew; and now the heavy rains and gusting winds. He prayed with a focused heart and mind. In the midst of darkness a deafening thunder roared and lightning flashed.

He cried: "God, I know you can't forgive me. Whatever you wish, I surrender everything to you!"

Then he heard: "Lester, trust God." And a huge lightning broke through the sky and hit the tree at its roots. He felt the intense heat radiated through him – that instead of burning him, it gave heat as comfort to his cold and weakened body. Mysteriously, it gave him strength. He felt that the tree was being blown afar by the strong winds and pouring rains. He said: "What is this God? Please forgive me. If I die in this fall, I accept your punishment which I deserved."

Years passed.....

There was not a single trace of Lester. The people had entirely forgotten him. God must have given him the ultimate punishment – death and hell – so others may not emulate him.

-------o-------

One sunny day, the townspeople were invited to a Sunday service. The speaker started his message:

"Years ago, I was an atheist. I hated any mention of God!"

And the speaker related an anecdote that somehow resembled the preceding story.

"As the tree which I was holding on was blown by the storm, it went down like a parachute. It fell on a swollen river which days before was dried up and filled with boulders of rocks. The tree served as my floater and drifted me to a distant place. From there I started a new life."

And he gave his concluding remarks. "My fellow folks please forgive me for all my shortcomings to you and to God. I am your long lost town mate. I'm your new pastor . . . Lester Cruz."

Love Has a Twist

The power of love is the sweetest experience we enjoy because it flows freely from God. In intricate ways He has grand design for each of us.

"God must have love and blessed this county," observed John as he was walking around with Peter, his host.

"Definitely," replied Peter. "The people here have long longevity averaging at age 97; our mortality rate is almost zero and we live in abundance," he boasted.

While they were dining in a restaurant fronting a street, a funeral procession passed by.

John said: "I thought you have almost zero mortality. I just arrived here an hour ago and you have this funeral procession?"

Peter replied: "Oh, yes. It confirms what I said earlier. This funeral is for a former rich businessman who died of depression."

"Why was he depressed?"

"Because of bankruptcy"

"What's his business?"

"He was the owner of the only funeral parlor in the county."

As they continued chatting another funeral procession passed by.

"What's this again? Almost zero mortality rate and this is the second death in just over an hour of my stay here. You're kidding, Peter!"

"No, I'm not! You see that person died of malnutrition or, simply put, hunger."

"You see, you're lying again. You told me you live in abundance here!"

Peter replied: "I'm not lying, it's true. That funeral is for a woman. That's the wife!"

Unlimited Love for God

Love knows no boundary. At times it transcends one's expectations. God shows to us love with no limit. Here is a story related by my high school friend about Anne and Joseph.

At a tender age of eighteen, they met at a party. They were very much attracted to each other.

Joseph said: "One day when we finish college, I'd like to take you as my bride."

She happily remarked: "That's my dream, too!"

But Joseph was an atheist while Anne was devoutly religious. And to make it harder for them, the parents of Anne were convinced about people ending up in divorce because of religious incompatibility. In fact, her father divorced his first wife because they didn't share the same religious beliefs. The dad told her about this and she realized the consequences that may happen to her and her beloved.

She told Joseph about this and he agreed, because of his great love for her, to become a Christian. He enrolled in a sectarian school. To the delight of Anne and of course Joseph, every day went smoothly as Joseph was transformed as a Christian.

Upon their graduation from college, both planned for their wedding. Friends were happy that two great loves will be united in holy matrimony soon.

Anne was the happiest woman on earth and so was Joseph.

The wedding day drew near.

One day, she received this call from Joseph: "I like to tell you something."

"I know, I'm excited. Our wedding is set and finalized already," replied Anne.

"I'm also excited Anne, because I am happy with God now. The wedding will have to go on though a little bit delayed, perhaps."

"What do you mean?"

"I'll be happy to officiate your wedding. I was already ordained as a priest."

God's Gift Rediscovered

When God created us, He made us complete "beings." Everything to live and enjoy life was "packaged" in each creation. But unfortunately many of us do not reach the full potentials of what the Creator designed us for. Is it because we don't appreciate much of what we are due to our environment or our limited mindsets? The "doing the best I could" is an appropriate phrase that should instead be our yardstick in the pursuit of our endeavors. "Whatever the mind could conceive, we could achieve" is a good adage that should be internalized in our system.

Here is a story of a cock fighter who dreamed of raising the most winning breed of fighter-roosters. He bought an egg of an eagle and put it in the nest to be hatched by a mother hen. Upon hatching, the young eagle grew with the other chickens in the breeder's farm.

The cock fighter expected that his roosters would acquire the good fighting traits and possibly the physical attributes from this eagle. But instead the reverse happened. The eagle could not kick hard and could not fully extend its wings.

One day a young pilot friend noticed this young eagle growing among the chickens. He bought it to develop it as a real eagle, the King of fowls.

The pilot went up the hill and threw the eagle upward to let him fly and glide. But it was so frightened that it flew only for few meters. The eagle was chickened.

After some time, the pilot climbed up a mountain and repeated it. This time the eagle was stronger and flew farther but went down again like a chicken.

After a week, the pilot flew his small fixed-wing plane and in the air he released the eagle.

The eagle was so scared that it forgot to open its wings. It was plummeting fast to its death. It looked for help from the pilot ... and there it saw the extended wings of the plane flying over.

The eagle was emboldened. It imitated the plane; extended its wings and glided. It stretched longer its wings and flapped them a little; and it soared! Excited by its new-found skill, the eagle soared and "played" with the plane in the sky.

The moral of the story: God created our bodies complete with ingredients to live and enjoy our lives. Let's utilize them to the fullest and, like the eagle, let's look at the sky as the limit (God created the sky too). If there is no way out, let's look up.

Ms. Eva Sevilla-Lee of Las Vegas, Nevada, a devout Christian follower, tries to decipher the enigma of God's dimensions and intentions as she writes:

"Of one thing I am sure, however: that not everyone can weigh the value of knowing God. One song, I can't trace the origin, had these endearing lines inserted:

"Who can weigh the value of knowing You?
Who can judge the worth of who You are?
Who can count the blessings of loving You?
And who can say just how great You are? "

"The existing broad category of believers currently covers those who are already enjoying the blessings of knowing Him. Others, not yet, or never. For no secret reasons, the faculty of the brain obligates us to approach God as His giftings provide. Sometimes, a simple song or a hurricane delivers His worth. Then His very nature, as Lord God and Savior, inspires in us to study the Scriptures which reveals His worth all the more. I admit, we may have some differences of opinions as to what exactly constitutes His worth. Nonetheless, there are new number of God's proofs of His creative powers and divine intentions. Be it an event or new mathematical formula! Every day they happen and are always welcome. But perhaps the most important reason for our failure to scientifically examine God's phenomena of creation, salvation and revelation is the excessive cares of this world. The complexities of life simply diminish the scientific mind, the faith, and the zest, thereby towing men wholesale to mediocrity. But to those who can judge and discover the worth of God, life becomes altogether more wondrous."

Epilogue

XIV

A candle loses nothing by lighting another candle

–Proverb

Recently, two incidents serve as litmus tests to the faith of the faithful: The DaVinci Code and the alleged finding that Judas Escariot did not really betray Jesus Christ.

The book and movie "The DaVinci Code" broke the alleged secrecy that Jesus Christ and Mary Magdalene were "married" and had a child. In the case of Judas, Jesus allegedly insinuated to him that he must "betray" Him; that this act of "betrayal" was the most important than what anyone of His disciples did. This was what Jesus desired (or God planned) so that His spirit will separate from the physical body to enable Him to ascend to heaven and join the Father.

Religious leaders are apprehensive that these could crack further whatever faith is left among the faithful; or these plainly blaspheme the Holy Trinity.

These things are happening in the present. Will there be more "revelations" or fictions that would further harm the image of God?

In my opinion, religious leaders should seek ways to further reinforce the faith of the faithful to make such beliefs unwavering and unshakable, steadfast and as solid as the "rock of ages."

My personal experience reinforces my faith in God. Whatever challenges or blasphemies may come, my roots are now planted in solid ground. Like a tree, it will grow and bear fruits no matter how many strong storms will try to bring it down.

Twelve years ago I was awakened at around three in the morning. I felt restless. Then an earthquake of around intensity five jolted my senses. Then it stopped. Quiet and calmness overcame my entire being. Relaxed, I hummed and noticed that it was a beautiful melody. I recorded the melody and immediately sat down and wrote the lyrics. With much ease I was able to compose the melody and lyrics in around two hours, as it seemed that an invisible angel was inspiring and guiding me. It was amazing because the lyrics jibe with the very core of this book – Creation, Punishment, and Existence of God – which I will write twelve years later! The lyrics also show the same substance and sequence: creation, punishment (Day of Judgment) and His existence (Second Coming). Is this a divine coincidence? This might as well be the theme song of this book.

For a person who has no musical education (I cannot read nor write musical notes) I did the reverse – composed music first, then lyrics. My wife requested her friend, Pastor Georgine Ness, a missionary of the Assembly of God for Asia-Pacific, to play the accompaniment. She graciously played and recorded it in early 1994.

As I sing it, it is therapeutic and reinforces my faith. I pray that it does the same for you. Here's the song:

The KING of Kings

I

The Lamb of God who meekly died for men
To save us and make us repent
Then multitudes have gratefully embraced
Jesus whom God has begotten

II

Humanities have flourished and progressed,
We prayed that our lives will be blessed
Yet still many are astray and misled,
They didn't care why He's resurrected

Chorus
Tribulations are in the offing
Signs show God soon is coming
As the Day of Judgment comes knocking,
Let us give our hearts to Him
(Instrumental then repeat I & Chorus)
Let us praise the King of kings

Primary Goal

How will this book be effective in reaching out to the nonbelievers?

As shown earlier, there are approximately 2.4 billion nonbelievers worldwide. With the kind of religions they embrace, many of these nonbelievers are situated in mainland China, its neighboring countries and other places of the world where the types of governance do not encourage religions; or where governments are basically materialistic like communism, dictatorships, and the like. But through modern technology in communications like the Internet and mass media (TV, radio, books, newspapers, etc.) spreading God's gospel with this added pragmatic knowledge may permeate through political, economic, social, religious, and intellectual barriers. Coupled with the religious missions of dedicated servants of God, this book has no limitations; it's transcendental.

As to how this book could be effective in making them realize that there is a creator, will also be based upon the level of literacy rates because, honestly, this book could be fully understood by those who have the basic knowledge of simple algebra. For countries whose peoples are mostly atheists but literate, this book could have great positive impact on their lives.

By and large, to the 6.5 billion people of the world, I offer this book which, when and if read conscientiously, will change their lives for more enlightened awakening.

What will be this book's primary goal? I am optimistic that people of the world will be more open and understanding to one another because we will be in the same level in thought, in word, and in deed in the name of our Creator or God. We will then be believing and speaking one verse for the universe – that humanity in the real sense is just ONE, a single group of intelligible creation, He truly treasures and loves.

Salient Lessons to Remember

In parting, let me highlight some salient lessons worth remembering.

* Just when a nonbeliever tried to spread his own "gospel" that "God is nowhere," God has intricate ways of changing things. The phrase turned to: "God is NOW HERE!"

*You read the significance of the "Divine Proportion" which is observed to be true in most creations, both animate and inanimate. The best application of the theory is the human face. The length and width of the forehead in relation to the dimension of the face conforms with this golden ratio; the dimension of the nose follows the golden proportion in relation to the nostrils; the length of the nose conforms with the overall length of the face; the length of the lips in relation to their thickness and width, etc. All of these proportions, to include most parts of the human body, are observed to be intricately designed. God must be meticulous in designing everything in us and in the universe!

*Do you strive for excellence in whatever things you do? How about giving more than 100%? In the mathematical and alphabetical presentation, the following is the score:

Knowledge- 96%
Hard work- 98%
Attitude- 100%
Love of God- 101%

"...while Knowledge and Hard Work will get you close, Attitude will get you there, it is the **Love of God** that will put you over the top!"

*The story of the eagle that rediscovered God's gifts. The bird was plummeting fast to its death. It **looked up** for help ... and there it saw the extended wings of the plane and imitated it. Then it soared like the King of fowls as it is supposed to be. The moral of the story: God created our bodies complete with ingredients to live and enjoy our lives. Let's utilize them to the fullest and like the eagle, let's look at the sky as the limit (God created the sky too). If there is no way out, let's **look up**.

pi is a universal constant which is the ratio of the earth's circumference to its diameter. It has a value of: 3.1415...85121215208919919715419165111914785 18591139318512054208

By decoding this in relation to their placement in the alphabet, it shows a message:

Hello. This is God speaking. Here I am. I created the universe.

or

Hello this is God speaking here. I AM. I created the universe.

*As a science grows, it generally takes a separate path from the mainstream of religion. However, these divine equations showcase that both religion and science could grow and flow together along a bigger and more dynamic mainstream of life of humanity, the way our Creator or God desired and designed them to be.

*As expressed in the parables and stories in this book, important evidence that God exists is His power to bestow upon His creations, especially humans, the sense of moral values. From this emanates CONSCIENCE which enables humans to discern what are right and wrong, good and bad. More important is His power to develop in humans that potent and mystical emotion of all – LOVE. The Power of Love becomes the strongest driving force for living creations to survive through millions of years, to keep on living, enjoying life and experiencing the wonders and ecstasy of procreation. Without these, living creations would just wither away and die; and the world will deteriorate and subsequently end. Who else could design these?

*As explained earlier, the Creator has two great powers. One is the power to create as represented by the equation, $C = I x a$.

When God fed 5,000 people out of 5 loaves of bread and 2 pieces of fish, the intensities of His power used were 500 *iop* and 2,500 *iop* for bread and fish respectively. He could feed more people should the situation warrant.

Second is His power to punish/destroy as represented by the equation, $a=C/I$. When He will punish these 2.4 billion nonbelievers on earth, He has at His disposal some 24 billion billion *iop* while the nonbelievers have a combined zero power to resist His might. Why do they have to wait for the Judgment Day to come and acknowledge Him? Why not now?

And last is the final equation, $I=C/a$ which shows His enormous hold in His domain. He has an intensity of power of 64 billion billion for humanity alone. If all His other creations are included, the greatness of His power is without any limit or boundary as reflected in the last line of the song, *"...Thy [enormous] power throughout the universe displayed..."*

*In the equation $C = I x a$, C and a must have the same unit of measure or the same species. If a is an ape, then the output C should also be apes. Not in any other way. This equation conforms with Genesis on Creation but mathematically and theologically refutes the Evolution Theory.

*The equation $I = C / a$ shows that a could not be zero but must be something. If a is zero as theorized by the Big Bang theorist, then the equation would not work. There must be something prior to the explosion. Who created this?

This equation therefore refutes the Big Bang Theory.

*We resist change and dwell too long on our comfort zones that new technology and knowledge are passing us by. The truism – Innovate or Stagnate – is a good reminder for us. Let us therefore join the bandwagon of unraveling more about God through faith and science as we travel beyond human horizon with Him.

These three divine equations define the identity and dimensions of the Creator in terms of His existence and power.

*In the *"Mystery of the Peanut,"* Dr. George Washington Carver "talked" to God asking about the mysteries of the universe. Instead, God answered him to concentrate on the peanut which is "something of his size." Dr. Carver thanked Him. God revealed to him the deeper secrets of the peanut from which the doctor came up with more than 200 useful products. After more than fifty years, we now enjoy the several food preparations of the mighty peanut.

From this story we learned a lesson: Let's leave the universe to God and humble ourselves as just peanut, then God will bless us.

Let us all remember that after all, He is the universe's Great Organizer and Designer whose acronym is **G.O.D.** Coupled with these divine equations defining His identity and dimensions, they show that He is real. Alive! Indeed, **GOD EXISTS!**

Bibliography

1. (part III) – The Need for Struggle, *1,000 Stories Vol. 1* Frank Mihalic p.23

2. (part III) – God's Presence, *1,000 Stories Vol.2* Frank Mihalic p.122

3. (part VII) – God's Part In Heaven, *1,000 Stories Vol. 1* Frank Mihalic p.189

4. (part VIII)- The Secret Life of Dust, *A History of the Small and Invisible*, Whole Earth, Fall 2002

5. (part XI) – One Hand of God, *Quote Magazine*, Ibid p.130

6. (part XI) – Delay, Ibid p.132

7. (part XI) – Mystery of Peanut, *1,000 Stories Vol. 2* Frank Mihalic p.73

Notes

1. Encyclopedia Britannica, *World Religions*

2. William Dembski and James Kushiner, *Signs of Intelligence* (Michigan, Brazos Press, 2001)

3. Walter Bradley, The *"Just So" Universe*

4. Stephen Meyer, *Word Games, DNA, Design and Intelligence*

5. Google (Internet), Ronnie Bryan – *Mathematical Proofs that God Exists*

6. *Creation and Evolution* (Torrance, CA, Rose Publishing, 1999)

7. *The Holy Bible*

Acknowledgments

I dedicate this to the 6.5 billion souls on earth that comprise the believers and the nonbelievers. To the believers, may your faith be reinforced; to the unbelievers, may this humble book open to you the path to your new beginning.

I acknowledge the wholehearted support of my wife, Aurora who helped me with my research. To my children – Donabelle, Eiscelle, Priscille, Claribelle with twin Clarinelle (daughters all!) who inspired me in the greatest spirit of Love. To all my grandchildren who made me recall and retrace my childhood – I could be young again.

To Angel D. Justiniano who gave me the full and unselfish support in the assembly and preparations of this book.

To the Ravina sisters – Lydia "Junko" and Tilly "Reiko" who motivated me and provided useful documents and advice; Lydia and Jenny Maglonzo who conscientiously did the editing.

To the mathematicians – Fredelina Pascua-Reyes, Pyng Urbano, Julian Lester Martinez and Clarinelle Duque-Esteves who reviewed the mathematical portion and gave valuable advice.

To the cover artists – Robert Paulino (Guam) and Patrick "PJ" Esteves (Spain).

To Pastor Jeni Ann Buensuceso Flores, Robert Paulino and Eiscelle Duque Paulino who reviewed the entire manuscript and provided valuable insights and analyses.

To the following who unselfishly gave their support and motivation: Pastors Cesar and Buenafe Aniceto, Pastors Manny and Wendy Calvo, Pastor Jess Soriano, Gen. Pablo Galvez (Ret.), Capt. Robert Bruce (Navy, Ret.), Atty. Ronnie Redila, and to all others who shall be supportive of this book's mission.

Patrocel N. Duque

Survey Form

Please fill this out before and after reading the book. You will find out the changes that you may have undergone if any. The question is: On a scale of 0 – 10 (0 is nonbeliever while 10 is strong believer), how strong is your belief in the Creator or God?

Name (optional)	Age	Sex	Religion or Belief	Nationality	Before Reading	After Reading

Comment(s):

_____

_____

_____

_____

_____

_____

- -

Fr: _____

_____

_____

Stamp

Mathematical Proofs
114 San Juan St.
Machananao, Dededo
Guam USA 96929